the AMAZING SPIDER-MAN

RED-HEADED STRANGER

SPIDER-MAN: RED-HEADED STRANGER. Contains material originally published in magazine form as AMAZING SPIDER-MAN #602-605. First printing 2009. Hardcover ISBN# 978-0-7851-4158-7. Softcover ISBN# 978-0-7851-3869-3. Published by MARVEL PUBLISHING, INC., a subsidiary of MARVEL ENTERTAINMENT, INC. OFFICE OF PUBLICATION: 417 5th Avenue, New York, NY 10016. Copyright © 2009 Marvel Characters, Inc. All rights reserved. Hardcover: $19.99 per copy in the U.S. (GST #R127032852). Softcover: $14.99 per copy in the U.S. (GST #R127032852). Canadian Agreement #40668537. All characters featured in this issue and the distinctive names and likenesses thereof, and all related indicia are trademarks of Marvel Characters, Inc. No similarity between any of the names, characters, persons, and/or institutions in this magazine with those of any living or dead person or institution is intended, and any such similarity which may exist is purely coincidental. **Printed in the U.S.A.** ALAN FINE, EVP - Office Of The Chief Executive Marvel Entertainment, Inc. & CMO Marvel Characters B.V.; DAN BUCKLEY, Chief Executive Officer and Publisher - Print, Animation & Digital Media; JIM SOKOLOWSKI, Chief Operating Officer; DAVID GABRIEL, SVP of Publishing Sales & Circulation; DAVID BOGART, SVP of Business Affairs & Talent Management; MICHAEL PASCIULLO, VP Merchandising & Communications; JIM O'KEEFE, VP of Operations & Logistics; DAN CARR, Executive Director of Publishing Technology; JUSTIN F. GABRIE, Director of Publishing & Editorial Operations; SUSAN CRESPI, Editorial Operations Manager; ALEX MORALES, Publishing Operations Manager; STAN LEE, Chairman Emeritus. For information regarding advertising in Marvel Comics or on Marvel.com, please contact Mitch Dane, Advertising Director, at mdane@marvel.com. For Marvel subscription inquiries, please call 800-217-9158. **Manufactured between 10/26/09**

Writers: **FRED VAN LENTE**
WITH **BRIAN REED (ISSUE #605, CHAPTER 3)**
Pencilers: **BARRY KITSON, ROBERT ATKINS,**
JAVIER PULIDO, LUKE ROSS
& **YANICK PAQUETTE**
Inkers: **RICK KETCHAM, BARRY KITSON,**
VICTOR OLAZABA, JOE RUBINSTEIN,
JAVIER PULIDO, RICK MAGYAR
& **MARK FARMER**
Colorists: **JEROMY COX, ANTONIO FABELA,**
JAVIER RODRIGUEZ, ROB SCHWAGER
& **NATHAN FAIRBAIRN**
Letterer: **VC'S JOE CARAMAGNA**
Cover Artists: **ADI GRANOV, STEPHANE ROUX,**
LEINIL YU & **MIKE MAYHEW**
Assistant Editor: **TOM BRENNAN**
Editor: **STEPHEN WACKER**
Executive Editor: **TOM BREVOORT**
Web-Heads: **BOB GALE, MARC GUGGENHEIM,**
JOE KELLY, DAN SLOTT, FRED VAN LENTE,
MARK WAID & **ZEB WELLS**

Collection Editor: **JENNIFER GRÜNWALD**
Assistant Editors: **ALEX STARBUCK** & **JOHN DENNING**
Editor, Special Projects: **MARK. D. BEAZLEY**
Senior Editor, Special Projects: **JEFF YOUNGQUIST**
Senior Vice President of Sales: **DAVID GABRIEL**

Editor in Chief: **JOE QUESADA**
Publisher: **DAN BUCKLEY**
Executive Producer: **ALAN FINE**

THE DB! FOR EVERY BRAND NEWS DAY!

THE DB

MAYOR JONAH JAMESON!!!

Mayor J. Jonah Jameson. Yes, THE J. Jonah Jameson is mayor of New York. How did it happen? When we last saw Jonah J. he was recovering from a heart attack and wondering what to do with his life now that his wife Marla sold the Daily Bugle out from under him to the king of slimeball journalism, Dexter Bennett. How did he turn it all around? Spidey couldn't tell you – he and the FF were busy quelling civil unrest in the Macroverse, a dimension who's time stream so differs from our own that a short mission cost them two months on Earth! And everyone knows two months in the life of Peter Parker, ANYTHING can change – his rent...

UNDER
UNDER
By Ben

What began as
unrelated ganglan
escalated to a full-
crime organizations
have seen their num

PETER PARKER'S P.O.V.

J. Jonah Jameson's mayor, my Aunt got married to his dad (so we're family now!), and I slept with my roommate, sparking World War Three (seriously – she chained up our fridge). And yet – these are the least of my problems.

Mary Jane Watson, the woman I was a hop, skip and web-sling away from I-thee-wedd-ing, is back in town. We haven't spoken much since she moved to LA, and then BAM! Right there, at the end of my Aunt's wedding, who's catching the bouquet? MJ. Sheesh.

Time to re-focus. I've been picking up freelance work for Front Line, but it's just barely covering the rent. I've got an in at City Hall now – my old pal from the Bugle, Glory Grant, is Jonah's new press secretary.

And my Spider-Sense is getting nervous – Doctor Octopus tentacled his way back into town. With that new Vulture a few weeks back and my scuffle with Hammerhead...maybe this is the start of a trend. Something's brewing on the horizon, I can feel it...

NOVEMBER 1997: AN EMPLOYEE OF A COMPANY OWNED BY OSAMA BIN LADEN WALKS INTO THE U.S. EMBASSY IN NAIROBI AND TELLS AUTHORITIES AL QAEDA IS GOING TO BLOW UP THE BUILDING.

NO ACTION IS TAKEN.

AUGUST 7, 1998: AL QAEDA BLOWS UP THE U.S. EMBASSY IN NAIROBI. 213 KILLED, MORE THAN 4,000 INJURED.

FEBRUARY 2001: AN ARIZONA FLIGHT SCHOOL REPORTS A SUSPICIOUS STUDENT, HANI HANJOUR, TO THE F.A.A. THEY BELIEVE HE MIGHT BE A TERRORIST.

NO ACTION IS TAKEN.

SEPTEMBER 11, 2001: 9/11 TERRORIST ATTACKS. NEARLY 3,000 KILLED, MORE THAN 6,291 INJURED. HANJOUR PILOTS THE PLANE INTO THE PENTAGON.

OCTOBER 2008: THE U.S. WARNS INDIA TWICE ABOUT AN IMMINENT MARITIME ATTACK ON THE TAJ MAHAL HOTEL AND OTHER MAJOR LANDMARKS.

NO ACTION IS TAKEN.

NOVEMBER 26-29, 2008: TERRORISTS ATTACK THE TAJ AND OTHER TARGETS IN MUMBAI. 173 KILLED, 208 INJURED.

YOU ARE SURROUNDED BY LISTENERS, GUARDIANS, WATCHERS.

THERE ARE EYES EVERYWHERE.

AND ALL OF THEM ARE BLIND.

RRRRRIIIIP

WHO-- PLEASE-- I--

YEAH, I GOT A CALLBACK FOR THAT IBSEN REVIVAL I TOLD YOU ABOUT.

"THAT IB-SEN RE-VI-VAL I TOLD YOU A-BOUT."

NO, MA, IT'S NOT A MUSICAL, IT'S IBSEN. "THE MASTER BUILDER."

"THE MAS-TER BUILD-ER."

THAT'S-- THAT'S MY VOICE!

CONVERSATIONS I HAD ON THE PHONE!

HOW DID YOU GET THAT?! YOU TAPING MY--

MA! C'MON...YOU KNOW I DON'T THINK YOU'RE STUPID!

"YOU KNOW I DON'T THINK YOU'RE STUPID!"

DON'T... DON'T START CRYING!

"DON'T... DON'T START CRYING!"

LOOK. I DON'T... I DON'T HAVE ANY MONEY TO GIVE YOU. I--I BARELY GOT A POT TO YOU-KNOW-WHAT IN!

YOU EVEN KNOW WHAT I DO FOR A LIVING? IT'S SO STUPID AND MEANINGLESS--

WHY DO YOU WANT TO KILL ME, MAN?

"WHY DO YOU WANT TO KILL ME, MAN?"

I'M NOTHING! A NOBODY!

"I'M NOTHING! A NOBODY!"

STOP COPYING ME!

"STOP COPYING ME!"

FFFFSSSSSS

YAAA--

GGGGGGGGGG!!

<

STILL, AUNT MAY'S NEW HUSBAND TOOK TIME OUT FROM HIS *HONEYMOON* TO EMAIL ME HE'D SET THIS *UP.* HE *KNOWS* HOW HARD UP FOR DOUGH I'VE BEEN!

THE *LEAST* I CAN DO IS MAKE AN *APPEARANCE.*

OF COURSE, THAT DIDN'T HELP ME *LAST NIGHT*-- I WAS ACTUALLY *EARLY* FOR MY *"DATE"* WITH MARY JANE, BUT SHE NEVER *SHOWED!**

GUESS THAT'S ALL I *DESERVE,* HAVING STOOD *HER* UP ALL THOSE TIMES WITH THE USUAL *SPIDEY* EXCUSES...IS SHE TRYING TO SEND ME A *MESSAGE?*

OR IS THE FACT ALL THE RESOURCES OF THE NEW YORK CITY POLICE DEPARTMENT ARE DEVOTED TO *BUSTING* MY BUTT JUST MAKING ME *PARANOID?*

🕷 LAST ISH, NATCH --*SHORT-TERM MEMORY STEVE*

AH, WELL.

THEY SAY YOU CAN'T *BEAT* CITY HALL.

GUESS I MIGHT AS WELL *JOIN* IT.

THAT WAS LIEUTENANT SINGH FROM THE *ARACHNID VIGILANTE TASK FORCE,* YOUR HONOR.

THE *WHAT?*

YOUR, UH, *"ANTI-SPIDER SQUAD?"* SPIDER-MAN *ELUDED* THEIR STING--

BLAST! BUT BUYING THAT OLD *S.H.I.E.L.D. JUNK* SURPLUS WAS *GENIUS!*

ACTUALLY, MR. MAYOR, ACCORDING TO THE LATEST *POLLING DATA...*

...VOTERS *LOVE* THAT IN THESE *TOUGH* ECONOMIC TIMES, YOU'VE MANAGED TO SAVE ENOUGH MONEY TO *BALANCE THE BUDGET.*

AH, MY BELOVED *CONSTITUENTS*...HOW I ADORE BASKING IN THEIR *APPROVAL*...

BUT...

...THERE *ARE* AREAS WHERE YOUR, AH, *FISCAL CONSERVATISM* IS *NOT* SO POPULAR.

YOUR NEGATIVES ARE *MUCH* TOO HIGH WHEN IT COMES TO *"PROTECTING THE CITY FROM TERRORISM"*--

WHAT? AFTER ALL I'VE *DONE* FOR THEM? *THE UNGRATEFUL S.O.B.'S!!!*

C'MON IN, PETE. WE'LL BE RIGHT WITH YOU.

HEY, GLORY. SO NOW YOU'RE *PRESS SECRETARY* TO HIZZONER?

"BAILOUT BOY" DEXTER BENNETT MADE WORKING AT THE D.B. SO BAD EVEN A *GOVERNMENT* JOB LOOKS GOOD, HUH?

DON'T YOU *KNOW* IT. I'VE ALWAYS HAD A BIGGER FLAIR FOR *MAKING NEWS,* ANYWAY...

"PETE." PETER. *PETER PARKER.*

OF COURSE. THE *WASTREL* AMONG THE MAYOR'S NEW *IN-LAWS*... HE WAS AT THE *RECEPTION...*

I'LL CALL YOU WHEN THE O.E.M. THING IS SET UP.

YES, MA'AM.

I *KNEW* THIS WAS A BAD IDEA.

I DON'T THINK I'M PHYSICALLY CAPABLE OF USING THE WORDS *"RESPECT"* AND *"J. JONAH JAMESON"* IN THE SAME SENTENCE.. EVEN IF IT *IS* FOR THE GOOD OF MY BELOVED NEW YORK!

FOR *WEEKS* I'VE PATIENTLY WAITED FOR THE BEST OPPORTUNITY TO PENETRATE THE MAYOR'S INNER CIRCLE.

AND, AS ALWAYS, THE ENVIRONMENT HAS *PROVIDED* ME WITH THE *PERFECT* ACCESS POINT.

FOR I *AM* THE ENVIRONMENT.

WHOA! SPIDEY SENSE ISN'T *TINGLING--*

I AM *INVISIBLE* BECAUSE I AM THE SAME THING YOU LOOK AT EVERY DREADFUL, DULL DAY.

--IT'S *POUNDING!*

I GOT A *CLEAR AND PRESENT* DANGER HERE!

EXCEPT, UH, FOR THE *"CLEAR"* PART...

WHO'S THE *BAD GUY* HERE? WHAT ABOUT THAT--

I AM THE DAY *BEFORE* YOU REALIZE EVERYTHING HAS GONE HORRIBLY, HORRIBLY WRONG.

TCK

NG

I AM THE CHAMELEON.

DAVE. CIVILIAN DID A HEADER. CALL PARAMEDICS?

SECURITY

LAIR SIX.

SKREEEEE

AND ALL OF THEM ARE BLIND.

CITY HALL IS LOCKED DOWN FAIRLY TIGHT THESE DAYS.

AUER, WALTER

VITATIS NOVI EBORACI

PERMIT FOR STREET PERFORMANC NEW YORK CITY

NOT THE EASIEST INTEL-GATHERING LOCATION.

JULY IV MDCCLXXVI

UNLESS YOU HAVE JUST THE RIGHT SPOT TO TRAIN A LASER MICROPHONE ON THE MAYOR'S OFFICE WINDOW TO PICK UP VIBRATIONS FROM THE GLASS.

NOW I HAVE EVERYTHING I NEED TO COMPLETE MY MISSION.

AND TEACH NEW YORK IT WILL NEVER FORGET...

...WHAT IT'S LIKE TO LIVE IN *FEAR*.

EXCUSE ME? PARDON ME? I HAVE A *QUESTION* ABOUT YOUR "COFFEE BEAN" COFFEE BEANS?

ARE THEY ORGANIC, BIRD-FRIENDLY, *AND* SHADE-GROWN?

I CAN'T *ABIDE* A LATTE WITHOUT A *SOCIAL CONSCIENCE*...

SORRY, WE'RE *CLOSED*. I THOUGHT I'D LOCKED THE--

MARY JANE!

YOU'RE BACK IN TOWN!

AND FOR *GOOD* THIS TIME, TIGER! MOTHERS AND H.A.M.M.E.R. DIRECTORS, LOCK UP YOUR SONS!

THIS IS *GREAT!* WHEN DID YOU GET IN?!

LAST FRIDAY, BUT I'VE BEEN IN NONSTOP REHEARSALS FOR THIS FASHION REALITY SHOW I'M HOSTING AT F.I.T.*

YOU'RE ONE OF THE FIRST OF THE OLD GANG I'VE HOOKED UP WITH!

REALLY? YOU HAVEN'T *SEEN*--

* FASHION INSTITUTE OF TECHNOLGY --*T.O.M.*

AH...

WHAT?

"YOU HAVEN'T SEEN *PETER?*"

SORRY, FORCE OF HABIT...

Menu

"OH, NO! DON'T *BREATHE* THE EX'S NAME! SHE'S SO *FRAGILE*, SHE MIGHT *BREAK!*"

YES, I'VE SEEN PETER. AND YES, IT WAS *WEIRD.*

I WAS AT HIS AUNT'S WEDDING-- I WAS SURPRISED I DIDN'T SEE YOU THERE!

AND NOW TO SEE YOU SLOP *MOP WATER* ALL OVER YOUR SHOES... TRYING TO PROVE THE BOSS ISN'T JUST SOME *TRUST FUND BABY?*

I'VE HAD TO **PITCH IN** A LOT LATELY. IT HASN'T BEEN EASY, UH...**RETAINING** STAFF...

AND...MAYBE YOU HAVEN'T HEARD...BUT THINGS HAVE BEEN A LITTLE... **DIFFICULT** FOR ME, LATELY...

I **HAVEN'T,** BUT I **WANT** TO HEAR ALL ABOUT IT.

I'VE DONE NOTHING BUT SLEEP AND REHEARSE FOR WEEKS!

C'MON, LET THE PROLES FINISH THIS IN THE MORNING.

TAKE ME TO THAT **CLUB DADA** ON 57TH! IT'S ALL L.A. WANTS TO TALK ABOUT.

DADA? THE COVER IS, LIKE, **FORTY BUCKS--**

A **BARGAIN** FOR GOOD TIMES WITH **OLD FRIENDS!**

MIND IF I FRESHEN UP FIRST?

I JUST **FINISHED** THE LADIES' ROOM...

NEVER FEAR! MY AIM IS...

...EXCELLENT...

HEY, GLORY. SO NOW YOU'RE PRESS SECRETARY TO HIZZONER?

HEY, GLORY.

RRRRRIIIP

SO NOW YOU-ARE-PRESS SEC-RE-TAR-Y TO HIZ-ZON-NER?

"BAILOUT BOY" DEXTER BENNETT MADE WORKING AT THE D.B. SO BAD EVEN A GOVERNMENT JOB LOOKS GOOD, HUH?

"'BAILOUT BOY' DEXTER BENNETT MADE WORKING AT THE D.B. SO BAD EVEN A GOVERNMENT JOB LOOKS GOOD, HUH?"

PLAY

PARKER.

PETER PARKER.

WHY DOES THAT NAME SOUND SO FAMILIAR TO ME?

TCH.

SO MANY NAMES.

SO MANY FACES.

AND I'VE BEEN THEM ALL.

GAAA—

FFSSSSSSSSS

CCCCCCCCCCC!!

MY.

FOR A SKINNY CHILD, YOU KICK LIKE A HORSE.

G... GGGG...

GOOD THING I GAVE YOU ENOUGH PROPOFOL TO KILL ONE.

H

KLUNK

SSHHHUUUU

BRR
BRR
BRR

BRR
BRR
BRR

M.J.?

I'M SORRY I MISSED YOU LAST NIGHT--BETWEEN THE JETLAG AND THE RECEPTION, I OVERSLEPT, I SWEAR.

MY TURN TO APOLOGIZE FOR STANDING YOU UP, HUH? HOW TIMES HAVE CHANGED...

BUT... HAVE YOU SEEN HARRY LATELY?

LOOKS LIKE HE'S GOING THROUGH TOUGH TIMES. I THINK...

PETER, I THINK HE'S SLEEPING IN THE COFFEE BEAN.

WE REALLY NEED TO DO SOMETHING TO HELP HIM.

SO CAN WE TRY THIS AGAIN? CONNECTING?

SSHHHUUU-CLANK

AMAZING SPIDER-MAN #603

PETER PARKER LIVED LIKE A **REFUGEE** WHO ROAMS FROM CAMP TO CAMP.

THIS IS ONE OF THE MORE **ANONYMOUS** BEDROOMS I'VE EVER BEEN IN.

HE MUST HAVE USED IT JUST TO **SLEEP**...

...AND SLEPT NOT ALL THAT **OFTEN.**

THIS IS ONE OF THE ONLY PERSONAL PHOTOGRAPHS I COULD FIND.

IF **YOU** ARE "M.J.," I VERY MUCH LOOK FORWARD TO **LUNCH.**

I ALSO DISCOVERED A PROFESSIONAL **CHEMISTRY SET** AND A CERTIFICATE TO TEACH **HIGH SCHOOL** IN THE STATE OF NEW YORK.

I THOUGHT HE WAS A **PHOTOGRAPHER.**

MAKE UP YOUR **MIND.**

PETE?

WE NEED TO TALK.

DINING ROOM. NOW.

I KNOW WHAT YOU'RE THINKING.

I THINK I MADE MY POINT WITH THE PADLOCK ON THE REFRIGERATOR, RIGHT?

I JUST... AFTER WHAT HAPPENED-- AFTER THE RECEPTION...

BUY YOUR OWN DAMN FOOD!

"HOW CAN HE POSSIBLY IMPERSONATE THIS MAN HE KNOWS NEXT TO NOTHING ABOUT?"

THAT'S A COMMON MISCONCEPTION ABOUT MY LINE OF WORK.

...I THINK YOU SHOULD GO. FIND ANOTHER PLACE. CAN WE SAY...TWO WEEKS?

POINT OF FACT, I DON'T NEED TO KNOW MUCH BEYOND THE BARE BASICS OF THE FACES I INHABIT.

THAT SHOULD GIVE YOU PLENTY OF TIME TO...

=MMPMF=

THE TRUTH IS, NONE OF US REALLY *KNOWS* ANYONE ELSE.

WHAT WE'RE *CAPABLE* OF AT ANY GIVEN MOMENT.

OH.

WE CANNOT SEE BEYOND OUR *OWN* LIVES AND DESIRES.

OTHER *PEOPLE*, WELL...

OH... PETER...THIS IS *BAD*...

...THIS IS *SOOOO BAAAD*...

=GIGGLE=

...THEY'RE JUST PART OF THE *BACKGROUND*.

WHOA.

WHAT?

YOU'RE ON TIME.

MORE THAN I CAN SAY FOR YOU.

NOT THE BLONDE.

BUT... *BETTER.*

I ALWAYS FACTOR IN "*PARKER TIME*" WHEN COMING TO MEET YOU.

YOU LOOK GOOD.

PETER PARKER, YOU *FASCINATE* ME.

OH, AND THANKS TO YOUR COLLAR I SEE *WHY.*

SHE ANYONE I *KNOW?*

ACTUALLY-- NO. NEVER MIND. IGNORANCE IS BLISS.

WE'RE HERE FOR YOUNG MASTER *OSBORN,* ANYWAY.

DID YOU KNOW HE *SOLD* HIS TOWNHOUSE? I THOUGHT HE HAD SOME MONEY OF HIS OWN, BUT--

WAIT.

"HARRY" IS HARRY *OSBORN?*

--HE ON THE OUTS WITH *STORMIN' NORMAN?* HE FINALLY GET CUT OFF?

HEIR TO THE DIRECTOR OF *H.A.M.M.E.R.?*

M.J.-- ...HOW COULD YOU NOT *KNOW?*

HOW COULD *ANYONE* NOT KNOW?

MISS WATSON!

AAAHH! AW, NO! COME ON!

JUST *TWO MINUTES* OF YOUR TIME! *PLEASE!*

WHO'S HE?

HE STARTED IN *L.A.* I CAN'T BELIEVE HE FOLLOWED ME *HERE*...MUST HAVE STAKED OUT MY SET!

HE'S...A LITTLE *FIXATED* ON ME. HE SAYS HE'S WRITTEN A SCREENPLAY FOR ME TO STAR IN...

IT INVOLVES *OUTER SPACE* SOMEHOW...

MAYBE WE CAN SLIP OUT THE--

NO. WAIT HERE.

YOU! COME HERE.

IT'S A FREE COUNTRY, I CAN GO WHERE I WANT!

LEGGO! STOP!

WHAT ARE YOU, HER BOYFRIEND?

WHO DO YOU THINK YOU ARE--

HMPF.

Star
Princess

a
screenplay
by
William
Hladek

SPLSSH

WHAT HAPPENED?

NOT A BAD GUY, REALLY. I THINK HE'LL LISTEN TO REASON.

EASY FOR YOU TO SAY.

LOOK. PETE. I DON'T WANT TO FIGHT.

I JUST WANT TO HELP OUR *FRIEND*, WHO I THINK IS NOW, BASICALLY, *HOMELESS*.

NO WORRIES, M.J. I'M ON IT.

CONSIDER HARRY OSBORN *TAKEN CARE OF.*

4:00 P.M.
GRACIE MANSION.

AN ENTIRE AFTERNOON-- **WASTED!** THESE PHOTOS ARE **WORSE** THAN USELESS!

THOMPSON LOOKS LIKE HE WANTS TO "FRAG" ME!

HE HAVE THE **POST-TRAUMATIC STRESS** OR SOMETHING?

I'LL FIX **HIM!** I'LL TAKE HIS **JOB** BACK!

YOUR HONOR...SPEAKING AS YOUR MEDIA ADVISOR...

...AND AS A **HUMAN BEING**...

...VENDETTAS AGAINST **PARAPLEGIC WAR HEROES** TEND TO BE POLITICAL **NON-STARTERS**...

BULL HOCKEY! IT WORKED **WONDERS** FOR **SAXBY CHAMBLISS!**

THE CORPORAL'S FILE SAYS HE'S A HUGE **SPIDER-MAN** FAN, SIR.

MAYBE YOUR "ANTI-SPIDER SQUAD" RUBBED HIM THE WRONG--

YES! THE ANTI-SPIDER SQUAD!

HAVE THEM MEET ME HERE AT ONCE!

OH, NO. YOU'RE NOT SENDING THEM AFTER THOMPSON...?

NO, YOU IDIOT!

AT **LAST!** IT CAME FROM STORAGE UPSTATE--

I CAN GIVE THE SQUAD A TAXPAYER-FREE UPGRADE TO THEIR **ARMOR!**

4:45 P.M.

THERE IT IS.

SHADOW COMMAND-- FROM THE OUTSIDE.

JUST ANOTHER UNASSUMING WAREHOUSE IN LONG ISLAND CITY.

WELL DONE, PETER PARKER.

I WAS ABLE TO DOUBLE BACK AND DETERMINE ITS LOCATION, THANKS TO YOU...

... AS WELL AS THE HOMING DEVICE I LEFT IN THE MEN'S ROOM.

I'LL TAKE ONE OF THOSE CELL PHONES TOO.

5:03 P.M.

I FOUND THE RIGHT ADDRESS. DELIVERY WILL BE MADE AT NOON TOMORROW.

FINALLY.

Quetta, Pakistan.

WE WERE BEGINNING TO THINK YOU HAD LOST YOUR NERVE.

THAT'S BECAUSE YOU'RE USED TO WORKING WITH BRAINWASHED ADOLESCENTS.

NOT PROFESSIONALS.

MAKE SURE THE SECOND HALF OF MY PAYMENT IS IN THE CAYMAN ACCOUNT BY TOMORROW, NOON, EASTERN STANDARD.

I WILL CHECK BEFORE COMPLETING THE TRANSACTION.

WHAT? THEN HOW DO WE KNOW YOU WILL FULFILL YOUR--

NO! THIS WAS NOT OUR ARRANGEMENT!

THAT WAS BEFORE YOU INSULTED ME.

I AM SORRY YOU ARE SO SENSITIVE. BUT I THINK I WILL REFUSE.

YOU ARE NOT THE ONLY ONE WITH OTHER NAMES, "CHAMELEON."

YOU DO NOT KNOW MY REAL ONE. OR MY FACE. OR WHO I REALLY WORK FOR.

YOU DO NOT EVEN KNOW WHERE YOU ARE CALLING NOW--

COLONEL.

LOOK BEHIND YOUR NANGAR PARBAT.

NOON.

TOMORROW.

MY MONEY.

≠KLIK≠

IF I HAD TO **GUESS** ...

SPLSH

U-STORE IT

...I'D SAY COL. KASAB AND HIS RENEGADE PRO-TALIBAN ELEMENTS IN INTER-SERVICES INTELLIGENCE ARE SOFTENING NEW YORK UP FOR A MUMBAI-STYLE MULTI-TARGET ASSAULT.

AS FOR *PETER PARKER*, PHYSICALLY *WEAK*, TORMENTED BY THE ATHLETES AT HIS HIGH SCHOOL, HE HAD HIS UNCLE, HIS ONE FORM OF *STABILITY*, TAKEN *VIOLENTLY* FROM HIM ...

... AND SO HE GREW INTO A *CHILD-*MAN, FLEEING *RESPONSIBILITY* AT EVERY TURN.

WOMEN, THE POOR CREATURES, ARE *DRAWN* TO THESE UNKNOWABLE PHANTOMS WHO FLIT FROM JOB TO JOB, BED TO BED ...

... BUT PARKER *SPURNED* THE LOVE OF THE ONE WOMAN WHO WAS CLEARLY THE BEST THING THAT EVER *HAPPENED* TO HIM.

AND HE HAD TO SUFFER THIS RICH TWIT *OSBORN*, WHO HAD THE *WORLD* LAID AT HIS FEET, BUT TURNED HIS *NOSE* UP AT IT.

LORD, HOW THAT MUST HAVE *GNAWED* AT YOU, PETER.

YOU, WHO WERE WELL ON YOUR WAY TO A POINTLESS LIFE OF *MEANINGLESS OBSCURITY* BEFORE I CAME ALONG.

BUT *NOW* THEY'LL REMEMBER YOU, PETER, IN THE *RIGHT* WAY.

THIS IS MY *GIFT* TO YOU.

ONE LAST ACT OF *MERCY*.

DING-DING

I THOUGHT I LOCKED THE--

BANG

HOW MUCH CAN YOU LEARN ABOUT A MAN'S LIFE IN A DAY?

BANG

BANG

I SAY...

BANG

RED-HEADED STRANGER:
DECONSTRUCTING PETER

...EVERYTHING.

FRED VAN LENTE WRITER	ROBERT ATKINS PENCILER	VICTOR OLAZABA INKER	JEROMY COX COLORIST	VC'S JOE CARAMAGNA LETTERER	TOM BRENNAN ASST. EDITOR	STEPHEN WACKER R.I.P.	TOM BREVOORT EXEC. EDITOR	JOE QUESADA EDITOR IN CHIEF	DAN BUCKLEY PUBLISHER	ALAN FINE EXEC. PRODUCER

GALE, GUGGENHEIM, KELLY, SLOTT, VAN LENTE, WAID & WELLS WEB-HEADS

AMAZING SPIDER-MAN #604

5:25 A.M.

THIS IS NOT GOOD.

YEAH, THAT'S IT, KEEP YUCKING IT UP, PARKER.

MAYBE IT'LL DISTRACT YOU FROM REALIZING HOW YOU WERE JUST A *HAIR'S BREADTH* AWAY FROM BITING THE *BIG ONE*.

STILL LIKE TO KNOW HOW CHAMMY GOT THE *DROP* ON ME.

NEXT THING I KNEW HE WAS TRYING TO *SUFFOCATE* ME, AND DROPPED ME DOWN INTO SOME KIND OF *PIT*.

EVEN THOUGH I WAS DRUGGED OUT OF MY SKULL, MY SPIDER-SENSE WAS STILL OPERATING ON A *SUBCONSCIOUS* LEVEL.

I WAS DIMLY AWARE OF THE SOUND OF RUSHING LIQUID--WHAT I *THOUGHT* WAS WATER...

...BUT TURNED OUT TO BE ACID!

INSTINCT KICKED IN, DRIVEN BY THE WARNING FROM MY SPIDER-SENSE.

MY SPIDER-STRENGTH LETS ME HOLD MY *BREATH* LONGER THAN THE AVERAGE HAPLESS VICTIM-- THAT'S WHY I WAS *ALIVE* IN THE FIRST PLACE.

AND HOWEVER LONG I WAS SUBMERGED, IT WASN'T ENOUGH TO COMPLETELY EAT THROUGH MY WEBBING...

...JUST *BARELY.*

I PASSED OUT AT SOME POINT. WHEN I WOKE UP, I FOUND MYSELF ON THE FLOOR OF THE PIT.

I HAD NO IDEA WHERE I WAS.

BUT I DIDN'T NEED *THE OFFICIAL HANDBOOK TO THE SPIDEY-VERSE* TO KNOW WHOSE *ADDRESS* IT WAS.

PETER PARKER BECOMES OFFICIAL PHOTOGRAPHER TO THE *MAYOR OF THE CITY OF NEW YORK* AND IS IMMEDIATELY TARGETED BY THE *CHAMELEON?*

YOU DON'T HAVE TO BE *JACK BAUER* TO FIGURE OUT WHAT CHAMMY IS AFTER--

--SHADOW COMMAND, THE CITY'S COUNTER-TERRORISM *NERVE CENTER!* I WAS SUPPOSED TO DO A *SHOOT* THERE RIGHT BEFORE HE NABBED ME!

IT'D HELP IF I KNEW WHERE ITS TOP-SECRET LOCATION ACTUALLY *WAS.*

WOULD THE CHAMELEON ACTUALLY USE--

SPIDER-MAN! POLICE!

YOU ARE UNDER ARREST!

UHHNNHH!

WHABAAAM

NO!!

YOU HAVE THE RIGHT TO REMAIN SILENT!

IF YOU GIVE UP THAT RIGHT, ANYTHING YOU SAY CAN AND WILL BE USED AGAINST YOU IN A COURT OF LAW!

NOT NOW, YOU TESTOSTERONE-FUELED IDIOTS!!

I'M TRYING TO SAVE Y--

YOU HAVE THE RIGHT TO AN ATTORNEY AND TO HAVE AN ATTORNEY PRESENT DURING QUESTIONING!

SO I WISH YOU COULD GET THIS THROUGH YOUR FLAT SKULL--

I LOVE THIS CITY TOO!

O.E.M.'S "SHADOW COMMAND" IS ABOUT TO BE COMPROMISED--MAYBE EVEN ATTACKED--AND ONLY I CAN STOP IT IN TIME--

IF YOU'D JUST GET OUT OF MY FRICKIN' WAY!!

I GOT A SHOT--

NO! DON'T RISK IT, EVEN WITH THEIR ARMOR ON!

YEAH! DISPATCH! SPIDER-MAN'S TAKING ON ONE OF US!

SEND EVERYONE DOWN HERE!!

SKREEEEEH!

Inside Shadow Command.

SIR, THEY'RE PRACTICALLY ON OUR DOORSTEP. SHOULD I DEPLOY OUR OWN FORCE OF--

NO WAY. MOTHER TERESA COULD BE GETTING MUGGED OUT THERE AND WE STILL COULDN'T GIVE AWAY OUR POSITION.

BUSINESS AS USUAL. LOOK-- TRILLO IS ON HER WAY IN.

OPEN UP THE MOTOR POOL FOR HER. QUICKLY, WHILE EVERYONE IS DISTRACTED BY THE SPIDER.

LISTEN TO ME!

ALL OF YOU ARE IN GREAT DANGER--

HE'S LYING TO SAVE HIS OWN SKIN! THAT'S HOW HE WORKS! FINISH HIM, UNMASK HIM--THEN THROW THE BOOK AT HIM!

N.Y.P.D.

POLICE

GREAT. ONLY ONE COP VEHICLE DOWN THERE IS COMPLETELY IGNORING ME AND--

12:03 P.M.

WAIT...

WAIT!!

CHAMELEON!!

SKRAAASSHHH

KREEEEEE

KRUNNCH!

N.Y.P.D.

TIME TO PACK IT IN, CHAMMY!

AGAINST ME YOU'RE A LITTLE OUT OF YOUR LEAGUE--

SKRRAANCH!

KAWOK

OW.

UUUFFF!

ALMOST...!

NO!

HEEL.

MISTER MAYOR-- I-IN HIS HAND--

A *BOMB* IS ONE OF THE ONLY THINGS THAT COULD MAKE MY SPIDEY-SENSE GO THIS HAYWIRE--

KRUUUNCH

THAT'S PUBLIC PROPERTY, YOU--

--MENACE--

OH MY GOD.

HE'S TELLING THE TRUTH! THAT'S A DIRTY BOMB!

GET THE CONTAINMENT TRUCK OUT HERE!

00:10

NOW!

5:07 P.M.

WHAT DO YOU MEAN, *THEY ALL RESIGNED?!* MY *ENTIRE* SPIDER-SLAYER SQUAD?!

THEY ALL SIMULTANEOUSLY PUT IN FOR TRANSFERS, YES.

YOU'RE MY DEPUTY MAYOR FOR OPERATIONS, HASKELL! YOU *DENY* THEM!

P.B.A. WON'T STAND FOR THAT. SPIDER-MAN JUST AVERTED A MAJOR TERRORIST INCIDENT-- ON THE HEELS OF SAVING THE CITY FROM *DR. OCTOPUS*--

PLEASE! THE WALL-CRAWLER WAS WORKING *WITH* THE TERRORISTS AND *FRAMED* THAT COP! A *CHILD* COULD SEE THAT!

GET *GLORY* IN HERE, WE'LL SEND OUT A *PRESS RELEASE*--

MR. MAYOR, IF I MAY.

THIS IS *NOT* THE DAILY BUGLE.

YOU CAN'T SIMPLY *PRINT* WHATEVER YOU *WANT* TO BE TRUE AND EXPECT PEOPLE TO *BELIEVE* IT. YOU NO LONGER HAVE THAT *LUXURY.*

DON'T YOU *LECTURE* ME--

I'VE BEEN IN GOVERNMENT FOR 40 YEARS. ALL *ANY* POLITICIAN *EVER* HAS GOING FOR HIM IS HIS *CREDIBILITY.*

SQUANDER YOURS, AND YOU WON'T GET IT *BACK.*

THIS IS MY LETTER OF RESIGNATION.

IF YOU WANT TO CONTINUE PUTTING PERSONAL VENDETTAS OVER THE GOOD OF THIS ADMINISTRATION... OVER *NEW YORK CITY*...

...I ASK YOU TO *ACCEPT* IT.

HRRM.

6:30 P.M.
MAY PARKER'S HOUSE, FOREST HILLS, QUEENS

I *SCOURED* THE AREA AROUND SHADOW COMMAND AND DIDN'T FIND A *TRACE* OF HIM.

SO HE'S FADED BACK INTO THE BACKGROUND--*AGAIN!* WAY TO GO, SPIDEY.

GREETINGS AND SALUTATIONS, VARIOUS AND SUNDRY *REILLYS!*

WOULD YOU GIVE A *COUSIN* A HOME-COOKED MEAL IN EXCHANGE FOR A STEADY STREAM OF *SNAPPY PATTER?*

CHAMELEON LEFT BEHIND THE *"MASK GUN"* WITH THE SPIDER-TRACER ON IT WHEN HE FLED.

I SO *DON'T* WANT TO RETURN TO *GENERALISSIMO MICHELLE*, ROOMMATE FROM HELL, RIGHT NOW.

HARRY! WHAT ARE YOU DOING HERE?

MAKING MYSELF AT *HOME*, JUST LIKE YOU SAID LAST NIGHT! THANKS AGAIN FOR THE KEYS, BUDDY--YOU'RE A *LIFESAVER.*

WHA-HUNH?

I *SWEAR:* DAD CUTTING ME OFF AND BOOTING ME OUT OF MY PLACE IS JUST A *MOMENTARY* SETBACK!

AS SOON AS I'M BACK ON MY FEET, I'M GONNA PAY YOU *BACK RENT* ON YOUR OLD ROOM! I *PROMISE!*

WE TOLD HARRY HE CAN STAY AS LONG AS HE *WANTS*, PETAH...

GO ON UP, BUDDY-- A *FRIEND'S* HELPING ME UNPACK!

OKAY...

I DID *NOT* TELL HIM TO DO THIS--IT MUST HAVE BEEN THE CHAMELEON...

...FOR...*SOME* REASON...

WHAT KIND OF *HAVOC* HAS HE WREAKED ON MY LIFE...?

HEY, HARRY, LOOK WHAT I UNEARTHED!

YOUR PHOTO ALBUM FROM OUR COLLEGE--

--DAYS...

HEY.

HEY!

MMMMMMM!!

HEY!

WOW.

TO WHAT DO I OWE THIS HONOR, MJ?

...FOR THAT IS HOW MY *HUSBAND* INTRODUCED US.

YOU REMEMBER MY HUSBAND, DON'T YOU, *DMITRI?*

KRAVEN THE HUNTER.

SPIDER-MAN *KILLED* HIM. NOW MY DAUGHTER AND I NEED YOUR HELP...

...TO *RETURN THE FAVOR.*

RED-HEADED STRANGER:
THE ANCIENT GALLERY

FRED VAN LENTE	BARRY KITSON	RICK KETCHAM & BARRY KITSON	JEROMY COX & ANTONIO FABELA	VC'S JOE CARAMAGNA	TOM BRENNAN	STEPHEN WACKER	TOM BREVOORT	JOE QUESADA	DAN BUCKLEY	ALAN FINE
WRITER	PENCILER	INKERS	COLORISTS	LETTERER	ASST. EDITOR	WILLIE FAN	EXEC. EDITOR	EDITOR IN CHIEF	PUBLISHER	EXEC. PRODUCER

GALE, GUGGENHEIM, KELLY, SLOTT, VAN LENTE, WAID & WELLS WEB-HEADS

Chapter One

The Bahamas.
Six Weeks Ago.

ROPE'S TOO LONG.

MY SIXTEEN YEARS OF EXPERIENCE, FIVE ACADEMY AWARDS AND TRIPLE-CHECKED MEASUREMENTS SAY *OTHERWISE*.

FROM *THIS* CROW'S NEST TO *THAT* TOWER WINDOW OVER THERE?

NO WAY.

C'MON, MARY JANE. WHY ARE YOU BUSTING MY CHOPS?

WHAT ARE YOU, AN EXPERT ON SWINGING FROM ROPES OR SOMETHING?

COR BLIMEY! YOU WAS RIGHT!

HOPE KEIF'S OKAY--HE'S BEEN ME STUNT DOUBLE ON ME LAST FOUR PICTURES!

I'LL BE IN MY TRAILER.

YOU GET THE MAIL I SENT OVER? ALONG WITH THE LAST COUPLE SCRIPTS?

YEAH, I'M GOING THROUGH IT NOW. THANKS, CRAIG.

ANYTHING PIQUE YOUR INTEREST?

'BOUT TIME TO START LINING UP YOUR NEXT PROJECT...

I'M SORRY, CRAIG, I CAN ONLY MAKE MY WAY THROUGH HALF OF MOST OF THEM.

IT'S THE SAME THING, OVER AND OVER AGAIN.

"SUPPORTIVE WIFE OF HERO."

"HOSTAGE WIFE HERO MUST RESCUE."

"DEAD WIFE HERO MUST AVENGE."

"CHEATING BITCH-WIFE HERO THROWS OVER FOR CO-STAR MORE FAMOUS THAN WIFE BY ACT THREE PLOT POINT."

EVERY CREDIT MIGHT AS WELL READ, "WITH MARY JANE WATSON AS 'THE GIRL.'"

I MEAN, IF I WANTED TO PLAY THE WIFE I WOULD HAVE STAYED IN NEW Y...

SPEAKING OF NEW YORK, THE PRODUCERS OF THAT "SEWN UP" SHOW CALLED AGAIN.

THEY DESPERATELY WANT YOU AS HOST, AND I DON'T BLAME THEM. WITH YOUR MODELING BACKGROUND, YOU'RE PERFECT.

arker
0 Ingram St.
Forest Hills, NY
11375

Mary Jane Watson
2500 Kurtzberg Way
Thousand Oaks CA
91359

REHEARSALS BEGIN AT F.I.T. IN MANHATTAN NEXT MONTH--

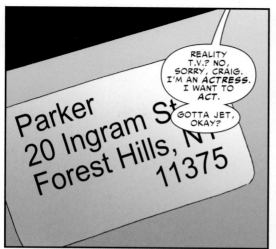

Parker
20 Ingram St*
Forest Hills, NY
11375

REALITY T.V.? NO, SORRY, CRAIG. I'M AN *ACTRESS*. I WANT TO *ACT*.

GOTTA JET, OKAY?

NOT PETER.

WHEW.

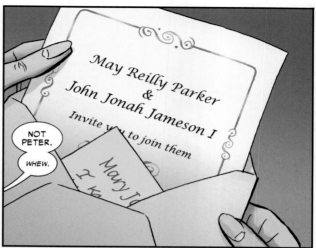

May Reilly Parker
&
John Jonah Jameson I

Invite y...u to join them

Mary J...
I k...

MARY JANE, I KNOW THERE'S A BIT OF *BAD BLOOD* BETWEEN YOU AND MAY, BECAUSE OF...THE WAY THINGS *ENDED*.

BUT ALL GUESTS TO HER *WEDDING* GET A *"PLUS ONE"*, AND I THOUGHT, WELL...

...SINCE MAY'S STARTING A *NEW LIFE*...

...THIS MIGHT BE THE RIGHT TIME TO PUT *OLD GRUDGES* TO REST...

WILL YOU BE ATTENDING?

YES ☐
NO ☐

SWEET- HEART! YOU SCARED THE...

YOU SAID *FATE FOUR* HAD TWO MORE WEEKS OF PRINCIPAL?

IT DOES-- BUT MY SHOOTING DAYS GOT MOVED AROUND SO I DECIDED TO COME HOME AND SURPRISE YOU...

WHAT ARE YOU DOING TO YOURSELF?

AWESOME! I'VE MISSED YOU SO MUCH!

I'VE GOT A SURPRISE FOR YOU, TOO!

THAT YOU'RE A BLONDE NOW? TOO LATE-- I KNOW.

ACTUALLY-- *YEAH!* I GOT IT, M.J.

ME. NOT PINE. NOT EFRON. NOT KITSCH.

BOBBY CARR IS PLAYING *STEVE ROGERS!*

THE DAY AMERICA DIED

By

Brian Lazarus

OH--*WOW*, TIGER! WOW! YOU KNOW, ON THE WAY OVER, I HAD THIS *FEELING*-- I KNEW YOU'D GET IT!

THIS IS MY TICKET OUT OF *"COMPLICATED TEEN HUNK"* PARTS AND INTO A-LIST ACTIONERS... WITH A ROLE THAT'S *CRACK* FOR ACADEMY VOTERS!

THEY LOVE HOLOCAUST VICTIMS, DISABLED PEOPLE AND DEAD *SUPER HEROES!*

WHO *DOESN'T?*

IT IS *MANDATORY* WE GO OUT AND *CELEBRATE.*

...AFTER THE *PRIVATE CEREMONY*, OF COURSE...

♪ WANNA BE YOUR SUPER HERO-- ♪

OH, CRA...

SORRY, BABE. THE STUDIO. GOTTA TAKE IT.

Incoming Call

YOU'RE KIDDING, RIGHT? YOU PEOPLE SPEAK ENGLISH?

I TOLD YOU. I'M WORKING ON IT. AND YOUR CONSTANT HOUNDING IS NOT HELPING--

U.S. Department of J...

Drug Enforcement Admin...

MISTER CARR.

DO YOU WANT TO GO TO PRISON?

DO YOU WANT US TO CALL EVERYONE FROM T.M.Z. TO TEEN BEAT TO COVER YOUR PERP WALK? NO?

THEN STOP STALLING AND ROLL US UP TO DOBSON. WE DON'T WANT YOU, WE WANT YOUR DEALER.

YOU DON'T UNDERSTAND MY POSITION. I'VE GOT TO BE SUPER-CAUTIOUS HOW I GO ABOUT THIS.

SHE'S GOT EYES EVERYWHERE IN THIS INDUSTRY--

--NOT TO MENTION SHE'S COMPLETELY PSYCHOTIC!!

MR. CARR. YOU DON'T SEEM TO UNDERSTAND YOUR POSITION...

"...I'M NOT THE GUY WHO TRIED TO SNEAK FIVE HUNDRED MILLILITERS OF *MUTANT GROWTH HORMONE* ONTO THE RED-EYE TO J.F.K. IN HIS *SOUL PATCH* GROOMING KIT."

SKREEEEEECH

IT'S ATTACHED!

GO ASK ALICE!

COAST IS CLEAR, BOSS.

THEY REMEMBERED WHAT THE DORMOUSE SAID.

GGKK

SHUK

WE'VE *DRILLED* THAT OPERATION TIME AND AGAIN.

IT *SHOULD* TAKE *SEVEN* SECONDS.

TK-TK-TK-KLIK

YOU TOOK *TWELVE.*

SO NOW I'M *LATE.*

WHA-BUMP!

KIDS, DON'T TRY THIS AT HOME.

I AM A *TRAINED* DAMSEL IN DISTRESS.

SIGH.

PLAYING THE GIRL.

AGAIN.

I AM NOW **THREE HUNDRED AND FORTY** SECONDS BEHIND SCHEDULE, THANKS TO YOU!!

TOTALLY UNACCEPTABLE!!

I HAVE CLIENTS TO SEE TONIGHT!!

NOW, ONCE AND FOR ALL--

...BUT IF YOU EVER FIND YOURSELF *IN A MOMENT* LIKE THAT...

...AND BELIEVE ME, YOU'LL *KNOW* IT WHEN YOU *SEE* IT...

...DON'T DO WHAT I DID.

WHICH WAS *NOTHING*.

BECAUSE I WOULDN'T WISH THIS FEELING ON MY WORST *ENEMY*.

LEAST OF ALL *YOU*, MARY JANE.

BRRRAAAAAP

WHAT? NO!

HURRY, BOBBY!

GINNY! WHAT ARE YOU DOING? TRAITOR!

KILL THEM BOTH!!

THAT WAS THE *WHITE RABBIT,* BOBBY! "UNAUTHORIZED PHARMACEUTICAL DISTRIBUTOR TO THE STARS!"

LISTEN--

I GO AWAY TO SHOOT A MOVIE FOR A *MONTH* AND YOU GET MIXED UP WITH--

LISTEN TO ME. THE COPS ARE GOING TO WANT TO QUESTION US, BUT YOU DON'T TELL THEM A *THING* UNTIL WE TALK TO MY *LAWYER,* GET OUR *STORIES* STRAIGHT--

WHY WOULD WE NEED TO--

I HAD NO CHOICE. THEY WANTED A SPECIFIC *BODY TYPE* FOR ROGERS! M.G.H. WAS THE QUICKEST WAY FOR ME TO GET THAT!

I HAD TO MAKE A LEAP! I'M GETTING TOO *OLD* FOR MY USUAL PARTS! MY CAREER HAD ALREADY STARTED TO *PLATEAU!*

YOU KNOW WHAT THAT'S LIKE!

PARDON ME?

HONEY. AW, GEEZ. LOOK, I DON'T WANT TO OFFEND YOU. I *LOVE* YOU. BUT...

...*CAPTAIN FATE FOUR?* SERIOUSLY?

THE *HALF-LIFE* FOR EX-MODELS IN THIS TOWN...

YOUR *WINDOW* IS *CLOSING,* THAT'S ALL I'M GONNA SAY. I ALREADY SAID TOO MUCH!

I SEE.

AND HOW LONG HAS MY... EMPLOYMENT POTENTIAL WEIGHED SO HEAVILY ON YOUR MIND?

SEE? *THIS* IS WHY MY THERAPIST SAID I SHOULDN'T TELL YOU ABOUT THE M.G.H.

"SHE SAYS THERE'S ALWAYS *TENSION* IN A RELATIONSHIP...

"...WHEN THE *ONE* PARTNER IS SO MUCH MORE *SUCCESSFUL* THAN THE *OTHER.*"

OH, *GREAT.* THEY *CAUGHT* HER...THAT'S JUST *GREAT!* NOW SHE'S GONNA SPILL HER GUTS...

THERE'S GOT TO BE *SOME* WAY TO *SPIN* THIS. I DIDN'T KNOW WHAT THE STUFF *WAS* SHE WAS GIVING ME...DIDN'T KNOW IT WAS *ILLEGAL*...

I'M SORRY, BOBBY, I...

I DON'T DO "SECRET IDENTITIES" ANYMORE...

HUH?

I'LL *CALL* YOU...

NO, M.J., COME ON!

WE GOTTA PRESENT A *UNITED FRONT* ON THIS!

MARY JANE!

COME BACK!

OKAY, SOUND? GREAT.

WE'RE SITTING DOWN WITH THE BEAUTIFUL AND TALENTED HOSTESS OF THE NEW SYNDICATED FASHION REALITY SHOW "SEWN UP"...

...DOUBLE-THREAT SUPERMODEL AND ACTRESS MARY JANE WATSON. THANKS FOR GIVING US A LITTLE BIT OF YOUR TIME, M.J.

THANK YOU SO MUCH FOR HAVING ME.

SO, YOU'RE BACK IN YOUR NATIVE NEW YORK TO BEGIN FILMING AFTER SOME TIME ON THE LEFT COAST. WHY THE CHANGE?

OH, YOU KNOW, ONCE I HEARD THE PREMISE OF THE SHOW, I FELT IT WAS JUST SO COMPELLING, I IMMEDIATELY TOLD MY AGENT I WANTED TO BE A PART OF IT.

YOUR ACTING CAREER WAS JUST STARTING TO TAKE OFF, THOUGH. ANY REGRETS, GIVING THAT UP?

NOT AT ALL. HONESTLY, THAT WHOLE SCENE...IT'S NOT REALLY "ME," YOU KNOW?

MY GREATEST CREATION HAS ALWAYS BEEN MARY JANE WATSON. THAT'S THE ROLE I WANT TO PLAY FOR A WHILE.

HA HA! WELL SAID.

THERE WAS SOME "PAGE SIX" TALK THAT A FAILED LOVE AFFAIR HAD SOMETHING TO DO WITH YOU LEAVING THE BIG APPLE IN THE FIRST PLACE. ANY TRUTH TO THAT?

WOW, YOU GUYS ARE GOOD.

THAT'S WHY WE GET THE BIG BUCKS.

WELL, YOU GOT ME.

BUT THAT'S ALL BEHIND ME NOW.

OR, I GUESS...BY COMING BACK, I AM PUTTING IT BEHIND ME NOW.

HOW SO?

"WHEN WE ESCAPE BAD SITUATIONS... SOMETIMES WE GO TOO FAR IN THE *OPPOSITE DIRECTION,* YOU KNOW?

"I'M A NEW YORKER. *THIS* IS WHERE MY HEART AND SOUL LIE. THIS IS WHERE I'M MOST *ME.* NOT L.A.

"I JUST DECIDED I WASN'T GOING TO LET ANYTHING KEEP ME AWAY FROM *MYSELF* ANYMORE.

"I GUESS WHAT I'M TRYING TO SAY IS...

"...I'M NOT GOING TO LET *ONE MOMENT* DEFINE MY ENTIRE LIFE."

...*as* "The Girl"

FRED VAN LENTE	JAVIER PULIDO	JAVIER RODRIGUEZ	VC'S JOE CARAMAGNA
WRITER	ART	COLOR	LETTERER

UNTIL IT *WASN'T.*

GOTTA MAKE YOUR *CURRENT* GIRLFRIEND INSECURE, TRYING TO MEASURE UP TO AN *EX* LIKE THAT...

NGGGH... ONE MORE TIME... ALL TOGETHER, NOW...

I DON'T HAVE A GIRL-FRIEND.

WHAT ABOUT THAT GIRL *MICHELLE,* WHO KEEPS TEXTING YOU AND CALLING YOU AND EMAILING YOU AND IM'ING YOU ALL THE TIME?

VMMM VMMM VMMM

SPEAK OF THE DEVIL...

MICHELLE IS JUST THE PITBULL WHO SLEEPS DOWN THE HALL FROM ME.

THERE. IT'S OFF. PEACE IN OUR TIME.

SHE IS *NOT*--NOR WILL SHE *EVER* BE--MY GIRLFRIEND.

PETER PARKER, YOUR GIRLFRIEND MICHELLE WANTS YOU TO CALL HER IMMEDIATELY.

PETER PARKER...

CUT! CUT!! WHO LEFT THE P.A. SYSTEM ON?!

THAT DOES IT!! I'M PUTTING A *FORK* IN THIS THING ONCE AND FOR ALL...

MROW! WH-CHTIK!

SHE'S *NOT* MY GI...

OH, I GIVE UP.

HE'S SEPARATING FROM THE OTHERS.

BUT STILL--THIS MAY NOT BE THE RIGHT TIME TO STRIKE. TOO MANY *INNOCENTS* AROUND.

LAST TIME I TRIED TO TAKE THIS DIRTBAG OUT, *BYSTANDERS* GOT CAUGHT IN THE CROSSFIRE. THERE WERE INJURIES.

I TRACKED THE REILLY CLAN TO FOREST HILLS, *QUEENS* FROM BOSTON.

I KNEW IT WAS ONLY A MATTER OF TIME BEFORE THEIR *BLACK SHEEP* TURNED UP.

HMMM...

I SWORE THEN I'D *NEVER* ALLOW THAT TO HAPPEN *AGAIN.*

AVENGING INNOCENTS--MY INNOCENT *FAMILY,* MURDERED BY BEN REILLY--IS *RAPTOR'S* WHOLE REASON FOR EXISTENCE!*

*RAPTOR MISTAKES PETER PARKER FOR HIS CLONE, BEN REILLY. BUT SINCE YOU READ ASM ANNUAL #36, YOU ALREADY KNOW THAT. RIGHT?--WACKERPEDIA

WHAT DO WE HAVE HERE?

The Apartment of Peter Parker and Michelle Gonzales.

WHERE HAVE YOU BEEN? WE'RE SUPPOSED TO HAVE DINNER WITH THE SENIOR PARTNER OF MY FIRM AND HIS--

I WAS OUT WITH THE SWEDISH WOMEN'S WATER POLO TEAM FOR ALL YOU KNOW, MICHELLE!

AND IT'D **STILL** BE NONE OF YOUR BUSINESS!

BECAUSE **WE ARE NOT DATING!!** WE WERE NEVER **DATING!!**

YOU KNOW, I'M GETTING A LITTLE **TIRED** OF YOUR GAMES.

GAMES? WHAT GAMES? GAME OVER! I'M TAKING MY BALL AND GOING HOME!

FIRST WE HOOK UP AT YOUR AUNT'S WEDDING RECEPTION, WHICH WE **AGREE** WAS A MISTAKE--*

IT WAS A MISTAKE! IT WAS A MISTAKE!

THEN, WHEN I TRY AND TOSS YOU OUT, YOU START SWAPPING SPIT WITH ME ON THE KITCHEN FLOOR--**

*ASM #601 ** #603 --THE LOVE EDITOR*

I CAN'T BELIEVE I'M GOING TO SAY THIS...

BUT AT THIS POINT...SCREW MY SECRET IDENTITY...

⇥SIGH.⇤ THAT WASN'T **ME**, MICHELLE!

I KNOW IT SOUNDS COMPLETELY INSANE...

...BUT YOU WERE **REALLY** MAKING OUT WITH THE **CHAMELEON.** A SUPER VILLAIN--A MASTER OF DISGUISE--POSING AS ME.

I'M **SORRY.** I SHOULD HAVE TOLD YOU THE TRUTH **SOONER.**

YOU HAVE *GOT* TO GET OVER THE M.J. THING.

CHUNK

I--

WHO--

WHIFF

WHAT?!

ASIDE FROM YOUR *DALLIANCE* WITH YOUR ROOMMATE...

...WHICH WAS A *REAL BAD* IDEA.

I DON'T REMEMBER THE LAST TIME YOU WENT ON A DATE.

YOU NEED A GIRL, M'MAN.

AND IT DOESN'T HAVE TO BE SOME LONG-DRAWN-OUT RELATIONSHIP, MR. COMMITMENT.

GOOD, HARRY. BECAUSE I DON'T WANT ONE OF THOSE.

THIS IS ABOUT MAKING YOU BE *NOT A LOSER.* SO LET'S GET STARTED.

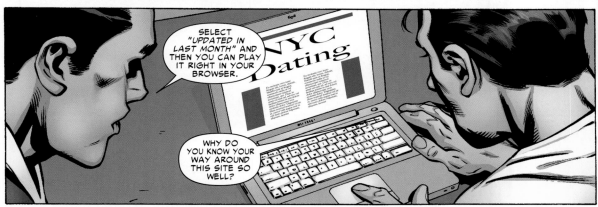

SELECT "UPDATED IN LAST MONTH" AND THEN YOU CAN PLAY IT RIGHT IN YOUR BROWSER.

NYC Dating

WHY DO YOU KNOW YOUR WAY AROUND THIS SITE SO WELL?

JUST PICK A GIRL.

WHERE DID YOU MEET LILY ANYWAY?

PARKER...

PICK. A. GIRL. ANY GIRL. PICK ONE AT *RANDOM* EVEN!

FINE.

KLIK

HI, EVERYONE. SANDY AGAIN.

I JUST GOT OUT OF ANOTHER RELATIONSHIP I THOUGHT WAS SERIOUS, BUT WASN'T.

I WAS IN LOVE, BUT HE DUMPED ME AND--

0:03 / 0:45

OH *NOOOO.* SHE WAS GIVING THE "MY RELATIONSHIPS ALWAYS END IN DISASTER" SPEECH. I'VE BEEN ON *THAT* DATE. IT'S NOT FUN.

OKAY THEN. NEXT GIRL.

KLIK

I BUY YOU A MEMBERSHIP TO A DATING SERVICE AND YOU CAN ONLY FIND GIRLS WHO TALK ABOUT THEIR EX-BOYFRIENDS?

IS THIS THE FAMOUS *PARKER LUCK*, OR DID YOU ACTUALLY TYPE "*BAD IDEA*" INTO THE SEARCH FILTER?

YAAAWN

MAYBE THIS WHOLE THING JUST ISN'T FOR ME, HARRY.

OH, MAN. *SUN'S* COMING UP.

I'VE GOT TO GET DOWN TO THE *COFFEE BEAN* AND GET THINGS OPENED.

SWING BY LATER?

NOT IF WE HAVE TO TALK ABOUT MY PITIFUL DATING LIFE.

PARKER! WHAT THE HELL ARE YOU DOING ON MY SIDE OF THE APARTMENT?

WE *DO*.

BUT I'LL LET YOU BUY ME LUNCH, SO IT WON'T BE ALL BAD.

AH, PARK AVENUE, I CAN ALWAYS COUNT ON YOU TO MAKE ME FEEL POOR.

I'M NOT SURE MY WALLET CAN EVEN AFFORD TO *SWING* PAST THIS PLACE, LET ALONE *WALK INSIDE.*

HEY, I CAUGHT THE GUY THAT STOLE THIS STUFF.

THOUGHT YOU MIGHT LIKE IT BACK BEFORE THE POLICE GOT HERE.

OH! THANK YOU!

THANK YOU!

JUST DOING MY PART TO MAKE NEW YORK--

I...

HI.

HI.

DID MY VOICE JUST CRACK?

YES.

ONCE AGAIN, THANK YOU SO MUCH.

WOW. YOU JUST SAT THAT DOWN, AND YOU DIDN'T EVEN CHECK TO SEE IF I STOLE ANYTHING.

IF YOU STOLE ANYTHING...

OUT OF THE BAG OF STOLEN THINGS.

NO, I MEAN-- MOST PEOPLE ASSUME I'M HIDING SOMETHING BEHIND THE MASK, AND SO I'M PROBABLY A CROOK RUNNING A SCAM PRETENDING TO BE A SUPER HERO.

YOU'RE NOT?

WHICH PART?

THE, UM, HIDING SOMETHING UNDER THE MASK PART.

OH. UM, WELL, ASIDE FROM WHO I AM?

NO.

OH MAN OH MAN OH MAN...

ARE YOU OKAY?

I'M TRYING REALLY HARD TO FIGURE SOMETHING OUT...

NO, IT WOULD BE SILLY--

YOU WANT TO KNOW HOW TO ASK ME TO HANG OUT AND NOT REVEAL YOUR SECRET IDENTITY?

I...

WHAT IS IT?

I OWE YOU BIG TIME FOR GETTING THIS STUFF BACK.

MAYBE I CAN HELP?

YEAH, ACTUALLY.

WELL, MAYBE WE COULD MEET SOMEWHERE TONIGHT?

WEEOOOOO WEEOOOOO

OH, HEY, THERE'S THE POLICE SIRENS.

I SHOULD PROBABLY SKEEDADDLE.

HOW ABOUT THE TOP OF THIS BUILDING? NINE O'CLOCK?

FINE JEWEL

I'LL BE THERE!

HEY, PETE.

HEY. SORRY I'M LATE. YOU GET LUNCH YET?

NOT YET.

CHRIS, I NEED YOU TO COVER FOR ME.

YOU BROWSE THE DATING SITE ANY MORE?

NO, AUNT MAY. I'VE BEEN BUSY.

YOU? BUSY?

YEAH! WEIRD, HUH?

I MEAN, MY HAVING A LIFE AND EVERYTHING.

BUT YOU WILL BE PLEASED TO KNOW, I MIGHT HAVE MET A GIRL.

IS THAT A FACT?

CLOSE ENOUGH.

TOO EARLY TO SAY ANYTHING MORE THAN THAT THOUGH.

OF COURSE IT IS.

GO GRAB A SEAT. I'LL BE READY FOR LUNCH IN JUST A MINUTE.

OH! SO SORRY! EXCUSE ME!

OH! HI, DANIELLE.

HI? UM...

HAVE WE MET?

GAH!

OH! NO... NO. I'M JUST...UH...

REALLY GOOD AT GUESSING NAMES?

OOOKAY...

...FREAK...

I CAN'T *BELIEVE* I'M DOING THIS.

GOING ON A *DATE* AS SPIDER-MAN?

DO *SUPER HEROES* GO ON DATES AS *THEMSELVES?*

ASIDE FROM *JOHNNY STORM,* I MEAN.

OH NO...

I'M BECOMING JOHNNY STORM!

I EXPECTED *SO MUCH MORE* FROM MYSELF.

THERE SHE IS.

I DON'T HAVE TO GO DOWN THERE. I COULD TOTALLY *BAIL* ON THIS MEETING AND BREAK HER HEART.

WHAT'S *ONE MORE* PERSON IN NEW YORK THAT HATES SPIDER-MAN, RIGHT?

BUT I FELT SOME SORT OF *CONNECTION* WITH HER AT THE STORE EARLIER.

AND THEN I BUMPED INTO HER AT THE COFFEE BEAN...

I'M NOT ONE TO BELIEVE IN *SIGNS* AND *PORTENTS*--

(I *DON'T EVEN KNOW* WHAT A *PORTENT* IS, NOW THAT I THINK ABOUT IT...)

OK, PARKER. STOP TALKING TO YOURSELF. GO DOWN THERE AND SAY--

I COULD... I MEAN IF YOU *WANT*...WE COULD SWING AROUND?

ON A *WEB*?

YEAH. I'VE BEEN TOLD IT'S FUN.

OCCASIONALLY, YOU EVEN GET SHOT AT.

I'M ACTUALLY PRETTY SCARED OF HEIGHTS. STANDING ON THE ROOF LIKE THIS IS KIND OF PUSHING IT TO THE LIMIT.

MAN, THOUGH, CHRIS WON'T BE ABLE TO *BELIEVE IT* WHEN I SAY I TURNED DOWN A WEB-SWING.

CHRIS?

YEAH. MY BOYFRIEND.

YOU-- YOU HAVE A *BOYFRIEND*?

YEAH.

DOES HE KNOW YOU WERE MEETING ME TONIGHT?

YEAH!

REALLY?!

YEAH! HE'S WORKING LATE AT THE COFFEE BEAN ACROSS TOWN.

AND HE'S *OKAY* WITH US HANGING OUT?

OF COURSE! I MEAN, IT'S *NOT* LIKE THIS IS A *DATE* OR ANYTHING.

RIGHT. HA! CRAZY THOUGHT.

ACTUALLY, HE ASKED IF I'D GET YOUR AUTOGRAPH.

MATCH.CON

BRIAN REED writer
YANICK PAQUETTE pencils
MARK FARMER inks
NATHAN FAIRBAIRN colors
VC's JOE CARAMAGNA letters

The End

AMAZING SPIDER-MAN #602 70TH ANNIVERSARY FRAME VARIANT
BY MIKE MCKONE

AMAZING SPIDER-MAN #603 70ᵀᴴ ANNIVERSARY FRAME VARIANT
BY MIKE MAYHEW

CHAMELEON

REAL NAME: Dmitri Anatoly Smerdyakov Kravinoff
ALIASES: Dr. Ashley Kafka, Dr. Turner, J. Jonah Jameson, Torpedo, Rick Jones, Dr. Henry Pym, Peter Parker, Captain George Stacy, Dr. Robert Bruce Banner, General Thaddeus Ross, Captain America, Kraven the Hunter, Spider-Man, Professor Newton, others
IDENTITY: Secret
OCCUPATION: Professional criminal, freelance spy; former crimelord, servant
CITIZENSHIP: Russia
PLACE OF BIRTH: Russia
KNOWN RELATIVES: Nikolai Kravinoff (father, deceased), Sonya Smerdyakov (mother, deceased), Sergei Kravinoff (Kraven the Hunter, half-brother, deceased), Vladimir Kravinoff (Grim Hunter), Nedrocci Tannengarden (nephews, deceased), Alyosha Kravinoff (Kraven the Hunter, nephew)
GROUP AFFILIATION: Formerly Exterminators, Sinister Twelve, Sinister Six
EDUCATION: Unrevealed
FIRST APPEARANCE: Amazing Spider-Man #1 (1963)

HISTORY: Dmitri Smerdyakov was the illegitimate son of the patriarch of the Russian Kravinoff family and a servant. His only friend growing up was Joe Cord, an American boy who once saved his life while his half-brother Sergei, the legitimate heir, and his father treated him with contempt and brutality. This scarred Dmitri so deeply that he repressed his very identity and came to believe he had been friends with Sergei instead. His loss of self led him to become a master of disguise and a Soviet spy. Initially without super-powers, the Chameleon relied on his skills and a mixture of costumes and make-up to conceal his identity. He wore a multi-pocket disguise vest in which he kept the materials he would need to mask himself at short notice.

In his first known appearance, Chameleon impersonated Professor Newton, a government scientist, to steal half of some missile defense plans. He then sent a message to Spider-Man (Peter Parker), electronically contacting him via his spider-sense, requesting a meeting and implying a profitable venture. Chameleon disguised himself as Spider-Man, though, and stole the second half of the plans, making his escape just as the real wall-crawler showed up. Spider-Man was at first framed for the theft but managed to bring Chameleon back to the police. Chameleon disguised himself as a police officer, scaring Spider-Man off by siccing the other cops on him. Spider-Man left the scene, thinking he had failed, not realizing that he had torn Chameleon's police uniform, allowing the cops to see the phony Spider-Man outfit underneath.

Chameleon was deported back to Russia, but returned soon after, having given up being a spy, and turned instead to a life of crime. Stymied again by the wall-crawler, Chameleon invited his half-brother, now known as Kraven the Hunter, to America to capture Spider-Man. The duo worked together, with Chameleon even dressing as Kraven to fool Spider-Man. Ultimately, though, both were defeated and deported by freighter where they bribed a sailor to set them loose in a lifeboat near Long Island. They came ashore right by Tony Stark's munitions factory and Kraven was quickly captured by Iron Man. Chameleon concealed his presence but decided to prove his superiority over Kraven by defeating the armored Avenger. Disguising himself as Captain America, Chameleon contacted Iron Man and convinced him that he was the real Cap and that the Cap at Avengers Mansion was really Chameleon. Iron Man and Cap fought it out until Giant-Man (Henry Pym) captured Chameleon and revealed the truth.

Chameleon quickly escaped prison and went to work for the Leader as his top lieutenant. The Leader sent him to New Mexico to learn the secrets of the Hulk. There, Chameleon impersonated General Thaddeus "Thunderbolt" Ross and Dr. Bruce Banner, stole a grenade-size gamma bomb and took Betty Ross as a hostage. Realizing he couldn't escape, Chameleon set off the bomb, which was smothered by the Hulk, dampening the blast. Though caught in the rubble, Chameleon survived and escaped, remaining in the Leader's employ until his boss' supposed death.

Chameleon next encountered Spider-Man after taking the place of Captain George Stacy who had been hired to protect a valuable art exhibit at the Midtown Museum. Peter Parker and Stacy's daughter Gwen were there and noticed that the Captain didn't seem to recognize them. After the exhibit was stolen and Stacy found drugged back at his apartment, Peter realized the Chameleon must have been involved. He persuaded Joe Robertson to plant a story in the Daily Bugle about a transfer of bonds and trapped Chameleon trying to steal them. Chameleon tried to escape through disguise but made the mistake of impersonating the one person Spider-Man knew to be a fake: Peter Parker.

The terrorist organization Hydra arranged for Chameleon's escape from prison so that he could impersonate Dr. Henry Pym and steal Pym's research combating their biological weapon Virus Nine. Pym, as Ant-Man, teamed with the Hulk and thwarted Chameleon, though it appeared at the time that Chameleon had murdered Bruce Banner. Later, Chameleon impersonated Spider-Man, attempting to free his friend Joe Cord from the New York Men's Detention Center. Accidentally striking the Hulk with his car, Chameleon quickly disguised himself as Hulk's friend Rick Jones and convinced the green goliath to break Joe out of jail. However, in a battle with police, Joe protected Chameleon from gunfire and was killed.

Designing a new costume that could instantly duplicate any clothing, Chameleon went back to crime. He was pursued after a jewel heist by Torpedo (Brock Jones) and Daredevil. His quick-changes failed to help him since Daredevil tracked him by his heartbeat. His next costume innovation used a holographic belt that stored the appearances of people he came into contact with and allowed him to take on their look. In one encounter, he managed to convince people that Spider-Man had attacked an old lady, leaving the wall-crawler's newly restored reputation in tatters. Later he obtained further powers by using a serum that could let him change his appearance at will. This liquid actually allowed his skin to be flexible enough to shift its appearance into any disguise Chameleon desired. He tried to kidnap a top scientist but was again thwarted by Spider-Man.

Chameleon then set his sights on ruling the New York underworld. He kidnapped publisher J. Jonah Jameson, impersonating him him in a long-term bid to influence events through the Bugle, and formed an alliance with Hammerhead. The Kingpin of Crime was embroiled in a power struggle with the werewolf Lobo Brothers. Chameleon and Hammerhead tried to instigate a full-on gang war, from which they would pick up the pieces. Chameleon, posing as Jameson, injected Spider-Man with a potion that left him unconscious for several days. Recovering, Spider-Man went after Jameson and discovered he was the Chameleon all along. Hammerhead and Chameleon's plans continued as they ambushed the Lobo Brothers and Kingpin during peace talks. After carving up the city into territories they each agreed to control, their alliance collapsed and their influence waned.

Soon after, Chameleon took the guise of Dr. Turner and persuaded Spider-Man to subject himself to a machine that supposedly would analyze his spider-powers. The machine, designed by the Tinkerer, ended up temporarily removing the wall-crawler's abilities instead. After discussing it with Mary Jane, Spider-Man decided to have his powers removed permanently. Now powerless, Spider-Man was attacked by Tarantula (Luis Alvarez) and Scorpion and needed the Black Cat's help to survive. Changing his mind, Spider-Man searched for Dr. Turner, eventually realizing he was actually Chameleon, by which time his powers returned naturally.

The Chameleon's next big plan was set up by the Green Goblin (Harry Osborn) before his death. The Goblin persuaded Chameleon to create two robots that would appear to be Peter Parker's dead parents in an effort to get Peter to tell them who Spider-Man really was. The Goblin already knew Spider-Man's identity but wanted to mess with Peter's head so he convinced Chameleon that Parker, due to all the photos he had taken, was sure to know Spider-Man's identity. When Spider-Man discovered the fraud, he went crazy with rage and disappointment at losing his parents again. The Chameleon escaped to Kraven's old mansion while Spider-Man hunted him down. Faced with a more fearsome and vicious Spider-Man than ever before, Chameleon's repressed memories of his unhappy childhood with Sergei returned and he fell into a coma-like state.

The Chameleon was taken to Ravencroft Institute but escaped after assuming the identity of his doctor, Ashley Kafka. He kidnapped Spider-Man and unmasked him, finally understanding why Spider-Man had been so mad after discovering the robot parents. Chameleon imprisoned Peter and convinced him he was a writer named Herbert Smith who was incarcerated in an insane asylum. Chameleon then took on the role of Peter himself but was foiled by Mary Jane, armed with a baseball bat, who knew her husband too well to fall for the impersonation. Escaping, he was shot by his nephew Alyosha Kravinoff, who said there could only be one Kravinoff in the world. Chameleon again barely survived. Later, he arranged to meet Spider-Man on top of the Brooklyn Bridge, wanting to make up for his crimes. There, he tried to commit suicide by jumping. Spider-Man blamed himself for this apparent death but Chameleon somehow survived.

Chameleon was a new addition during a gathering of the Sinister Six, formed as part of an elaborate, yet ultimately failed plot to destroy Spider-Man and gain immeasurable wealth by destroying the world's monetary system. He was later recommitted to Ravencroft. Following a time he believed himself to be Sergei, Chameleon joined Norman Osborn's short-lived Sinister Twelve after Osborn coerced Spider-Man into liberating him from prison. Members of the Avengers and Fantastic Four rescued Spider-Man and defeated the Twelve. When Spider-Man publicly revealed his secret identity as part of the Superhuman Registration Act, Chameleon formed a team called the Exterminators who distracted Spider-Man at Liz Allan's home while he, disguised as Peter, targeted Aunt May.

May detected the guise and drugged the Chameleon with cookies laced with sleeping pills. Chameleon no longer knows Spider-Man's secret identity; a bargain Spider-Man made with the demon Mephisto eliminated all knowledge of Peter Parker's dual identity. After Spider-Man publicly revealed his secret identity as part of the Superhuman Registration Act, Chameleon formed a team called the Exterminators who distracted Spider-Man at Liz Allan's home while he, disguised as Peter, targeted Aunt May. May detected the guise and drugged the Chameleon with cookies laced with sleeping pills.

Art by Keith Pollard

Art by Todd McFarlane

Art by Steve Ditko

HEIGHT: Unrevealed
WEIGHT: Unrevealed
EYES: Brown
HAIR: Unrevealed

ABILITIES/ACCESSORIES: The Chameleon can instantly change his appearance and imitate others so convincingly that practically no one can tell the Chameleon and his victim apart. His natural talents are now augmented with a face-changing serum. The Chameleon often employs masks, a multi-pocket disguise vest, a special costume that instantly duplicates clothes and a holographic belt.

POWER GRID	1	2	3	4	5	6	7
INTELLIGENCE							
STRENGTH							
SPEED							
DURABILITY							
ENERGY PROJECTION							
FIGHTING SKILLS							

Text by Mike Fichera